YOUR PET DOG

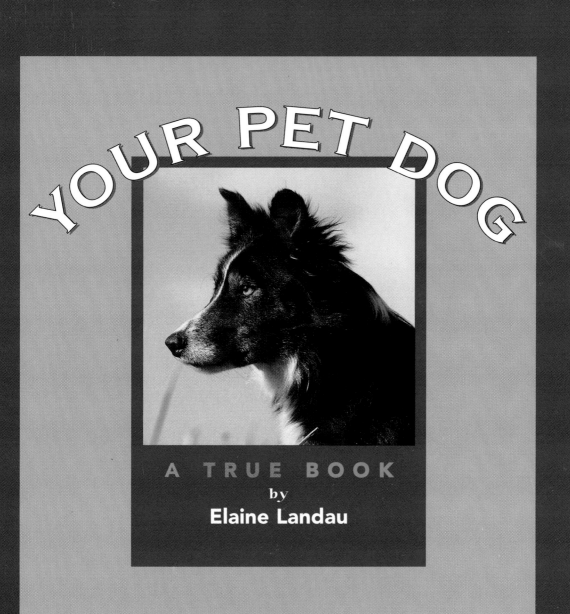

A TRUE BOOK

by

Elaine Landau

Children's Press®
A Division of Grolier Publishing

New York London Hong Kong Sydney
Danbury, Connecticut

Reading Consultant
Linda Cornwell
*Learning Resource Consultant
Indiana Department
of Education*

*Author's Dedication:
For Jerry, Bianca,
and Abraham*

A sled dog
in Alaska

Library of Congress Cataloging-in-Publication Data

Landau, Elaine.
   Your pet dog / by Elaine Landau.
      p.   cm. — (A True book)
   Includes bibliographical references and index.
   Summary: A simple introduction to choosing and caring for a pet dog.
   ISBN 0–516–20382–7 (lib. bdg.)   0-516-26263-7 (pbk.)
   1. Dogs—Juvenile literature. [1. Dogs. 2. Pets] I. Title. II. Series.
SF426.5.L365 1997
636.7'0887—dc21   97–15627
                                                       CIP
                                                       AC

Contents

A dog can bring
smiles and laughter.

A Dog of Your Own

Few things in life are more fun or more rewarding than having a dog. A dog can bring smiles and laughter and be a loyal friend.

Owning a dog is a wonderful thing—and a big responsibility. From the day you bring it home, the animal is yours to care for. You will have to make sure your pet always has food, fresh water, and medical care. And, of course, a dog needs plenty of love and affection. Also, if you are getting a puppy, it will have to be trained.

So before you choose your dog, think about these questions:

Are you really willing to take the time to care for a dog? You will be feeding and

Dogs require daily care.

walking the animal every day. This means you'll have less time for the other things you like to do.

Does your family want you to have a dog? Will they help take care of the animal when you can't be there?

Is your family
ready to help
you care for
a dog?

Does your family have
enough time, space, and
money to keep a dog?

If you answered yes to all
these questions, you may be
ready for a dog of your own.
But remember that your
animal's health and happiness
will depend on you.

Choosing a Dog

Before you actually choose your pet, you will probably have some idea of the kind of dog, or breed, you want. It may be a breed of dog you saw in a movie or on television. Or perhaps a friend, relative, or neighbor has a dog you like a lot.

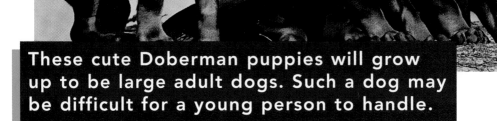

These cute Doberman puppies will grow up to be large adult dogs. Such a dog may be difficult for a young person to handle.

It is important to pick the right kind of dog for you and your family. Everybody loves a cute little puppy, but some little puppies grow up to be huge 150-pound (68-kilogram) creatures. A very large dog costs a lot to feed, and it is not likely to do well in a small apartment.

Do you want a purebred or a mixed-breed dog? A pure-bred dog's ancestors are all of the same breed. If you get a purebred dog, you may

These are purebred Dalmatians.

know in advance some of the characteristics the dog is likely to have. A mixed-breed dog's ancestors are of several different breeds. Their adult characteristics may be more difficult to predict, but mixed-breed dogs often live longer, healthier lives than purebred dogs. And they are usually gentle animals. Also, you can probably get a mixed-breed dog free or for very little money from your local

Mixed-breed dogs such as this one usually make gentle, healthy pets.

humane society or animal shelter. In many cases, you will be saving the puppy's life by adopting it.

If you want a purebred dog, the American Society for the Prevention of Cruelty to Animals (ASPCA) recommends getting a puppy from a reliable breeder. The ASPCA strongly discourages buying a puppy from a pet store. These puppies are more likely to have health and temperament problems.

Older purebred dogs can be gotten from rescue societies, which find new homes for abandoned purebred dogs. You can get a list of rescue societies, or of people who breed the type of dog you want, from a local dog club or the American Kennel Club.

If you are thinking about a purebred dog, learn about the breed you would like to own. Breeders and people who already own the type of

Labrador retrievers such as this one are gentle and intelligent animals.

dog you are considering can be good sources of information. Learn about the dog's temperament and adult size. Does it like children? Can a young person easily handle that kind of dog?

If you decide on a mixed-breed dog, ask what breeds the dog is a mixture of and learn all you can about those breeds. This information may tell you something about what the animal will be like.

This mixed-breed dog is part collie and part keeshond.

Do you want a male dog or a female? Some dog owners claim that females are more gentle and less likely to stray. But others insist that it depends on the individual animal.

These golden retriever puppies are too young to be parted from their mother.

Never bring a puppy home until it is at least eight weeks old. Before then it is too young to leave its mother. Don't choose a puppy that looks sick—watery eyes, a runny nose, or fever are signs of illness. It is difficult to tell much about the character of a very young animal, but don't pick a dog who seems too high-strung or snappish or one who seems too shy or fearful.

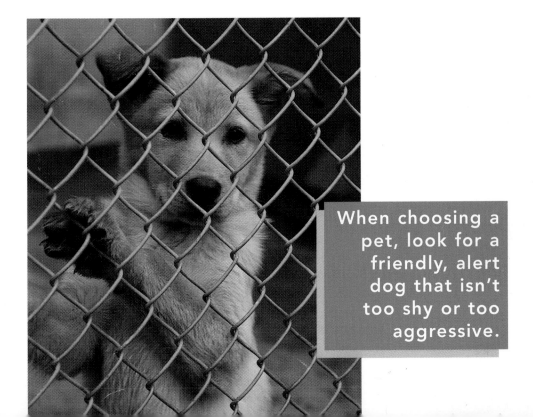

When choosing a pet, look for a friendly, alert dog that isn't too shy or too aggressive.

Doctors for Dogs

Apart from you and your family, a good veterinarian is your dog's best friend. Take your dog to a veterinarian soon after you bring it home. Your dog will need a checkup, as well as several vaccinations to protect it from infectious diseases. Bring your pet back to the veterinarian for yearly checkups. At these times, some of the vaccinations will need to be repeated.

The veterinarian can answer all your questions about your pet's care. If your dog becomes ill between checkups, take it to the veterinarian right away.

Supplies

Every new dog owner needs some basic supplies. Be sure to get these items before you bring your pet home.

Nutritious food and fresh water are essential to your dog's well-being. Many different types of dog foods are available, and some are made especially for puppies. These products include dry foods, semi-moist packaged foods, and canned foods. Your breeder or veterinarian can tell you which foods are best for your dog at various stages of its life. Do not feed your dog table scraps, sweets, or food meant for other pets. Never give a dog chocolate or alcohol—even small amounts of these can be extremely harmful to your pet.

Every dog should have its
own dishes for food and
water. Keep these bowls
clean—you wouldn't want to
eat from a dirty dish, and your

dog shouldn't have to either. Feed your dog the same amount of food every day at the same time. Puppies are usually fed four times a day, while older dogs eat only once or twice daily.

A dog should have a clean comfortable bed for resting and sleeping. A cardboard box lined with a thick, soft blanket is fine for a puppy. Try placing one of your old shirts in the box with the blanket.

Make sure your dog has a comfortable place to rest and sleep.

Don't wash the shirt first; the puppy will be comforted by your scent during the night. Beds for older dogs are available in pet stores and animal supply outlets.

You will need a collar and leash for walking your dog. Attach the proper identification tags to your pet's collar. These include the dog's city license and rabies vaccination

Get a proper leash and collar before you bring your dog home.

This dog's ID tags will help ensure its safe return if it gets lost.

tags, as well as an ID tag with your name, address, and phone number. In unexpected circumstances, any pet can stray, even those of responsible pet owners. If your dog is ever lost or injured, its ID tag can help ensure its safe return.

You will need a brush to keep your dog's coat and skin healthy. The type of brush you should use varies according to the dog's breed and

Long-haired dogs need careful brushing.

Dogs should be bathed about once a month.

the texture of its coat. Ask your veterinarian or breeder what type is best for your dog. Most dogs should be brushed at least three times a week, although daily grooming is best. Dogs generally should not be bathed more than once a month.

If you thought toys were just for kids, think again. Dogs need their own toys to play with. Puppies chew continuously while they are growing teeth, and having a chew toy makes them less likely to gnaw on your furniture.

Every puppy should have at least two toys—a hard rubber squeak toy to chew and a

toy made of knotted, sterilized rope for tugging and wrestling. Dogs can get bored, especially when they are home alone. Dog toys provide a healthy outlet for the animal's pent-up energy.

House-Training

If you get an older dog, it will probably be house-trained already. But a puppy must learn to relieve itself outdoors. House-training a puppy takes a great deal of time and patience.

While being house-trained, the puppy should be restricted

to one area of the house. Keep its bed and its toys in the same area. As this is the dog's living space, the animal will not want to soil it. When the puppy begins sniffing around for a place to relieve itself, take it outside immediately. Stay with the animal until it has finished, and praise your dog each time it relieves itself outdoors.

Never scold, shout at, or punish your puppy if it has an

Frequent walks are an important part of house-training.

accident indoors. You should expect such accidents when you are house-training a puppy.

Puppy Play

Plenty of exercise and fresh air are crucial to your dog's health. A big dog needs longer walks than a small one, but all dogs love their outings.

Exercising with your pet need not be limited to walks, however. Throwing a ball, frisbee, or rubber toy for your dog to fetch is fun for both of you.

Behavior and Training

A well-behaved dog is easier to care for and lots more fun to have around. You can find inexpensive obedience classes in most locations. In these classes, your dog will learn to follow simple commands such as "sit" and "stay." You can encourage its good behavior

A well-behaved dog
is easier to care for.

Your dog will learn to obey simple commands in an obedience class.

if you remember the following tips:

• Be consistent. Don't laugh when your dog jumps up on somebody and then get annoyed when it does the same thing the following day.

• Be upbeat. Praise—not punishment—is your best training tool.

• Pay attention to your dog's needs. A dog can't talk, but its posture and behavior often tell you how it feels. Learn to "listen" to your dog.

Learn to recognize how your dog is feeling.

Respect your dog's needs and feelings. This will help create a strong and lasting bond between you. A dog is not a toy you can toss aside when you are tired of it.

Proper dog care often takes lots of time and energy, but the rewards are great. You will have the boundless love of your new best friend.

Your dog will reward your care with boundless love.

To Find Out More

Here are some additional resources to help you learn more about dogs:

 **Books**

Alexander, Sally Hobart. **Mom's Best Friend.** Macmillan, 1992.

Calmenson, Stephanie. **Rosie: A Visiting Dog.** Clarion Books, 1994.

Manson, Ainslie. **A Dog Came Too: A True Story.** A Margaret K. Elderberry Book, 1993.

Patent, Dorothy Hinshaw. **Hugger to the Rescue.** Cobblehill Books, 1994.

Petersen-Fleming, Judy. **Puppy Care and Critters.** Tambourine Books, 1994.

Ring, Elizabeth. **Performing Dogs: Stars of Stage, Screen, and Television.** Millbrook Press, 1994.

Ziefert, Harriet. **Let's Get a Pet.** Viking, 1993.

Organizations and Online Sites

Acme Pet
http://www.acmepet.com/

Includes useful information on dogs including tips on choosing a dog, finding a breeder, grooming, and general care.

American Kennel Club
51 Madison Avenue,
New York, NY 10010
phone: (212) 696-8200
fax: (212) 696-8299
http://www.akc.org/

Sponsors dog shows nationwide and publishes official descriptions of the breeds they recognize. Their site includes information on dog breeds, listings of local AKC societies, AKC news, and a schedule of events.

American Society for the Prevention of Cruelty to Animals (ASPCA)
424 East 92nd Street
New York, NY 10128-6804
(212) 876-7700, ext. 4421
http://www.aspca.org/

This organization is dedicated to the prevention of cruelty to animals. They also provide advice and services for caring for all kinds of animals.

Dog Owner's Guide Home Page
http://www.canismajor.com/dog/guide.html

An excellent online publication for all dog owners or people considering a dog as a pet. Includes a valuable section on choosing the right dog complete with descriptions of many breeds. Provides information on dog sports, manners and training, and a section on kids and dogs.

rec.pets.dogs FAQ Homepage
http://WWW.Zmall.Com/pet/dog-faqs/

This Web site includes lists of questions and answers about dogs and dog care.

Important Words

breeder a person who mates dogs to produce a specific breed of dog

humane society an organization dedicated to the protection of animals

infectious a disease that can spread from one animal to another

rabies a deadly disease spread by animals

stray to wander far from home

temperament an animal's nature or disposition

vaccination the injection of a substance that protects an animal from a specific disease

veterinarian a person trained to medically and surgically treat animals

Index

Meet the Author

Elaine Landau worked as a newspaper reporter, children's book editor, and youth services librarian before becoming a full time writer. She has written more than ninety books for young people.

Ms. Landau lives in Florida with her husband and son.